COMPUTER
PIONEERS

Steve Jobs

Founder of Apple Inc.

Sarah Machajewski

PowerKiDS
press.

New York

Published in 2017 by The Rosen Publishing Group, Inc.
29 East 21st Street, New York, NY 10010

First Edition

Editor: Caitlin McAneney
Book Design: Mickey Harmon

Photo Credits: Cover, pp. 1, 3–32 (background) yxowert/Shutterstock.com; cover (Steve Jobs) SHAUN CURRY/Stringer/AFP/Getty Images; p. 5 David Paul Morris/Stringer/Getty Images News/Getty Images; p. 7 https://commons.wikimedia.org/wiki/File:Apple_Garage.jpg; p. 9 https://en.wikipedia.org/wiki/Heathkit#/media/File:HeathkitAA141w-19710220.jpg; pp. 11, 13 Tom Munnecke/Contributor/Hulton Archive/Getty Images; pp. 15, 17 Bloomberg/Contributor/Getty Images; p. 19 Ted Thai/Contributor/The LIFE Picture Collection/Getty Images; p. 21 Michael L Abramson/Contributor/Archive Photos/Getty Images; p. 23 Chris Polk/Contributor/FilmMagic/Getty Images; p. 24 https://en.wikipedia.org/wiki/Think_different#/media/File:Apple_logo_Think_Different_vectorized.svg; p. 25 Gilles Mingasson/Contributor/Hulton Archive/Getty Images; p. 27 Justin Sullivan/Staff/Getty Images News/Getty Images; p. 29 Featureflash/Shutterstock.com.

Library of Congress Cataloging-in-Publication Data

Machajewski, Sarah, author.
 Steve Jobs : founder of apple inc. / Sarah Machajewski.
    pages cm. — (Computer pioneers)
 Includes index.
 ISBN 978-1-5081-4837-1 (pbk.)
 ISBN 978-1-5081-4771-8 (6 pack)
 ISBN 978-1-5081-4804-3 (library binding)
 1. Jobs, Steve, 1955-2011—Juvenile literature. 2. Apple Computer, Inc.—History—Juvenile literature. 3. Computer engineers—United States—Biography—Juvenile literature. 4. Inventors—United States—Biography—Juvenile literature. 5. Businesspeople—United States—Biography—Juvenile literature. I. Title.
 QA76.2.J63M33 2017
 621.39'092—dc23
 [B]
                              2015034430

Manufactured in the United States of America

CPSIA Compliance Information: Batch #BS16PK: For Further Information contact Rosen Publishing, New York, New York at 1-800-237-9932

Contents

Changing the World

Picture the following scenes: A woman in New York uses a computer to talk face-to-face with a friend in Tokyo. On a city bus, a teenager listens to music on a device he can fit in his pocket. You're woken up for school by an alarm clock that's actually a phone. Today, these situations are part of normal life, but they weren't always. Computers can do these things because of the **visionary** mind of Steve Jobs, the co-founder and late chief executive officer (CEO) of Apple Inc.

Steve Jobs didn't invent computers. He just changed the way people thought about them. Jobs pushed computers' capabilities to their limits. Then, he redefined them. Because of his **innovation**, computers that were once giant machines seen only in the workplace are now devices that help regular people do almost anything.

Steve Jobs, pictured here in 2007, holds the earliest version of the Apple iPhone. It's considered by many to be a device that changed the world.

Starting Young

On February 24, 1955, in San Francisco, California, a young, unmarried college student gave birth to a baby boy. She decided to place the baby up for adoption. A couple named Paul and Clara Jobs adopted the baby. They named their new son Steven Paul Jobs.

Jobs's parents were very involved in his life; his mother taught him how to read before he started school, and his father taught him skills that would be useful later in life.

Jobs and his father spent a lot of time together. His dad set aside an area of the garage that became Steve's workspace. He taught Jobs how to build things, take them apart, and put them back together. Jobs once remarked that these moments were good for him and taught him a lot.

Jobs's creativity began in his parents' garage, which is now an important place in computer history.

Early Confidence

The Jobs family moved to Mountain View, California, when Steve was five years old. Today, this town is in an area called Silicon Valley because it's the heart of the United States' computer and technology industries.

Living in this area meant Jobs was surrounded by tech-minded people from an early age. One such person was a neighbor named Larry Lang. Lang built electronics from pieces that came in kits. After observing Lang's work, Jobs took up these kits as a hobby.

Building the electronics kits made a deep impression on Jobs. It gave him an understanding of how electronics work, but it also taught him that it was possible to build anything he saw around him. This early confidence, gained through learning and exploring, would stay with Jobs throughout his life.

Larry Lang introduced Jobs to Heathkits, which became his childhood hobby. The device pictured here is one example of what Heathkit electronics offered in the 1960s.

Unconventional Learning

Steve Jobs was very smart, but he was also a troublemaker. When he was in fourth grade, his mischief led him to meet someone who had a great impact on his life. Mrs. Hill taught the fourth-grade advanced class, and she found a way to get Jobs excited about school again—she said she'd give him money and candy if he did well on his homework! This kind of **unconventional** learning made an impression on Jobs, who said he learned more that year than any other time in his education.

Meeting "Woz"

In 1971, when Jobs was in high school, he met Steve Wozniak. "Woz," as he was called, was a student at the University of California, Berkeley, who also had a knack for electronics. Jobs and Wozniak bonded over their common interest, which was unusual at a time when few people knew about computer programming.

After high school, Jobs enrolled at Reed College in Oregon. He dropped out after only six months. In 1974, he was hired as a video-game designer for Atari Inc., but left there soon after he started, too. Jobs traveled to India and studied a religion called Buddhism. Later that year, Jobs returned to California and reconnected with Woz. The work that followed changed the computer industry forever.

Steve Wozniak

Steve Jobs

Jobs's and Wozniak's first business venture was selling a device Wozniak designed called the Blue Box. This device allowed people to **hack** into phone lines without having to pay for long-distance calls. The men are pictured here in 1977.

The Homebrew Computer Club

After Jobs returned to California, he started going to meetings of a group called the Homebrew Computer Club, in which Wozniak also took part. Its members were people who shared the same love for and interest in computers. The meetings were designed for members to trade ideas and information. It was also a **forum** to talk about rumors in the computer industry, and show off new computer parts or members' own inventions.

At this time, computers were used mostly in businesses. They were big and expensive, and few were available to **consumers**. However, research labs were exploring the idea of personal computing. Jobs believed in that idea. He **envisioned** a world where computers did more than run numbers for businesses—he saw them in the homes of regular people.

California was the right place to be for a computer lover like Jobs in the 1970s. At this time, personal computing was just slightly more than an idea. Jobs was ready to make it a reality.

Planting Apple's Seeds

The Homebrew Computer Club was very important to the future of computers. It was during those meetings that Wozniak showed off a small computer he built. With only a few chips, a video screen, and a personal keyboard, the machine was designed for **hobbyists**—not to be used in business. Jobs was inspired. He felt this computer was the one that could bring computers into people's homes. Luckily, Wozniak shared this vision. The two teamed up and founded Apple Computers Inc. on April 1, 1976.

Jobs and Wozniak started their company with $1,300 of their own money. Working off Wozniak's original design, the pair designed Apple's first computer in Jobs's bedroom at his parents' house. It's said they built the very first model in his parents' garage. They named it the Apple I.

The Apple I consisted only of a **circuit board**, which is pictured here.

Raising Money

Jobs and Wozniak faced a challenge when they started their company: where would they get money to build computers? They pooled their money and received a nearly $50,000 order from a local computer store, but they still didn't have enough. Determined to succeed, Jobs went to a local parts supplier. He convinced the store to give them parts on **credit**, even though they didn't own anything they could put up as **collateral**. Wozniak said this happened because Jobs was "very persuasive."

Introducing the Apple I

The Apple I was introduced to the public in 1976. The computer, which was simply a circuit board, didn't have a monitor to display information or a keyboard to enter information. Users had to buy those themselves. However, the technology was innovative compared to what was available at the time. It allowed users to load computer programs from other machines. Unlike other computers, it didn't require extra circuit boards to display text.

Jobs and Wozniak's innovative computer sold for $666, and it appealed mostly to hobbyists. A store called the Byte Shop sold more than 200 units, and in the end, the company earned around $774,000 from sales of the Apple I. It was successful, but it didn't revolutionize home computing the way Jobs envisioned. However, it set the stage for the product that eventually did.

The Apple I's success opened many doors for the two young **entrepreneurs**. A former executive at Intel, a computer chip manufacturer, invested $250,000 in Apple. This allowed Apple production to move out of Jobs's parents' garage.

The Revolutionary Apple II

Personal computing changed forever in April 1977 when Jobs and Wozniak introduced a new computer at the West Coast Computer Faire in San Francisco. It was called the Apple II.

The Apple II was unlike any other computer at that time. The computer had a built-in keyboard and power supply, and it contained all the necessary electronics inside a slim, compact frame. It was the first computer that had color graphics, which means it was able to produce images in color. The Apple II also stood out for its ability to be customized, or changed to meet a user's needs.

Jobs marketed Wozniak's breakthrough technology as an "extraordinary computer for ordinary people," focusing on the computer's simplicity. It worked—Apple's sales skyrocketed from $7.8 million in 1978 to $600 million in 1981.

Jobs's vision for Apple and its products was to create a tool that could be used at home, school, or work. While Wozniak was the mind behind the technology, Jobs's natural ability to sense what people wanted made the Apple II extremely successful.

Setting the Standard

Jobs had a knack for being able to see the future of computer technology. In 1979, he visited a Xerox Corporation research center. He saw a personal computer with commands controlled by a point-and-click tool. It also had a video display that featured documents and programs. Jobs remarked in a 1995 interview that, "within 10 minutes...[he knew] every computer would work [that] way someday...It was so clear."

Jobs took that inspiration back to Apple. In 1984, he **debuted** another pioneering technology: the Macintosh computer. Users commanded the computer with a mouse, rather than typing out complex commands, which was how computers worked until then. It had folders, icons, and a video display. Marketed as "a computer for the rest of us," the Macintosh became the standard in home computing.

The Macintosh was very successful, but Jobs refused to make it **compatible** with products made by IBM, one of Apple's biggest competitors. Other Apple executives disagreed, which eventually led Jobs to leave the company.

Revolutionary Advertising

The Macintosh was known as much for its revolutionary advertising as it was for its innovative technology. Steve Jobs hired an advertising firm to make a commercial for the computer with one request—he wanted "to stop the world in its tracks." During the 1984 Super Bowl, an ad aired in which a woman, who represents Apple, rebels against a "**Big Brother**"-type figure, which is meant to represent a government keeping its people in the dark. The ad told consumers that Apple gave them the power of technology. Today, the commercial is iconic.

Telling Stories

Jobs left Apple in 1985 over disagreements about how the company should be run. He took his pioneering sensibilities with him and found himself in the world of animation. Jobs met George Lucas, the director of the popular *Star Wars* movies, in 1986. Lucas wanted to sell the technology company he'd founded that developed film-editing software. Jobs purchased the computer graphics division and created the company that would be named Pixar Animation Studios.

Jobs once said the goal of Pixar was to revolutionize computer graphics, but its vision was to tell stories. Almost ten years after Jobs' purchase, the company released the world's first computer-animated feature film—*Toy Story*. The movie was a huge hit, and Jobs became a billionaire. In 2006, the Walt Disney Corporation purchased Pixar for $7.4 billion.

Steve Jobs became a board member at Disney after it purchased Pixar. The studio went on to release many wildly popular movies, including *Finding Nemo*, *The Incredibles*, and *Brave*.

"Think Different"

In 1997, Jobs returned to Apple. The company was failing and many people believed it was headed for bankruptcy. Jobs used his connections to make a deal with Microsoft, a software company, to offer its products for Apple computers. Next, Apple introduced a personal computer called the iMac, which was the best-selling personal computer in 1998. Thanks to Jobs's efforts, the company made a profit once again.

Think different.

Think different.

The "Think Different" campaign changed how people viewed Apple. It made the company seem revolutionary and, more importantly, cool—something that helped increase sales.

Around this time, Jobs made the decision to roll out a historic marketing campaign called "Think Different." Those words appeared over black-and-white photographs of important visionaries who had changed the world. When paired with the Apple logo, it presented the company's computers as revolutionary. The marketing campaign was a great success!

iPad, iPhone, iCEO

Jobs became Apple's CEO in 2000. Jobs set his sights on a growing industry: digital media players. Apple launched iTunes, a music and video file program, in 2001. Free and easy to use, iTunes was one of the first programs of its kind.

Jobs hit another home run later that year when Apple debuted the iPod. The tiny music player changed how people listened to music. It allowed users to carry around 1,000 media files in a pocket-sized machine. The iPod is considered one of the most revolutionary products of the 2000s.

In 2007, Apple debuted the iPhone. The touchscreen device was a cell phone, iPod, and computer all in one. Apple sold 1.4 million iPhones in just three months, and it was named *Time* magazine's "Invention of the Year."

Steve Jobs launched Apple's most important products during the company's annual Macworld conference. His usual outfit of blue jeans, black turtleneck, and wire-rimmed glasses became almost as famous as the products themselves.

A True Visionary

In 2010, Jobs debuted the Apple iPad. This product launched the tablet industry and became Apple's fastest selling product ever. With the eyes of the world watching the launch, people noticed something else—Jobs didn't look healthy.

Unknown to many, Jobs had suffered serious health problems. He was diagnosed with cancer in 2003 and had a liver transplant in 2009. In 2011, in failing health, Jobs stepped down as Apple's CEO. He died on October 5, 2011, at the age of 56.

Steve Jobs was a pioneer not just for his technical skills, but for his ability to see the power of society's relationship with technology. His legacy is everywhere, from the computer in your home to the phone in your pocket. For his innovation and creativity, Jobs is remembered as a visionary.

Steve Jobs spent his life doing what he loved. He once said, "...the only way to do great work is to love what you do. If you haven't found it yet, keep looking. Don't settle. As with all matters of the heart, you'll know when you find it."

Timeline

February 24, 1955
Steve Jobs is born in
San Francisco, California.

1971
Jobs meets Steve Wozniak, his future
business partner.

April 1, 1976
Jobs and Wozniak found Apple
Computers Inc.

1976
Jobs and Wozniak introduce the Apple I.

1977
Jobs and Wozniak debut the Apple II.

1984
Apple debuts the Macintosh computer,
which becomes the standard for
home computers.

1985
Jobs leaves Apple over disagreements
over how the company should be run.

1986
Jobs buys the computer graphics division
of George Lucas's technology company.
He names it Pixar Animation Studios.

1996
Jobs returns to Apple as a consultant.
He helps make the failing company
profitable again.

1998
Apple debuts the iMac, the best-selling
home computer that year.

2000
Jobs becomes Apple's CEO.

2001
Apple becomes a pioneer in the digital
media market with the launch of iTunes
and the iPod.

2007
Jobs debuts the Apple iPhone at the
Macworld conference. The all-in-one
phone, Internet, and music device is named
Time magazine's "Invention of the Year."

October 5, 2011
Steve Jobs dies from complications of
pancreatic cancer when he is just 56.

Glossary

Big Brother: A term that's used to describe a person or organization that has total control over people's lives. It was first used in George Orwell's book *1984*.

circuit board: A thin board with electric circuits that are designed to perform a task.

collateral: Something that is promised to be given in exchange if somebody can't pay back a loan.

compatible: Able to work together.

consumer: A person who purchased goods or services.

credit: Money or goods lent to someone on the condition that they can pay it back at a later date.

debut: To introduce something to the public for the first time.

entrepreneur: A person who organizes and operates a business.

envision: To imagine as a future possibility.

forum: A place or meeting where ideas are exchanged.

hack: To use a computer to gain unapproved access to data in a system.

hobbyist: A person who does something for fun.

innovation: A new method, idea, or product.

unconventional: Not in line with what is typically done.

visionary: Thinking about or planning the future with imagination or wisdom.

Index

Websites

Due to the changing nature of Internet links, PowerKids Press has developed an online list of websites related to the subject of this book. This site is updated regularly. Please use this link to access the list: www.powerkidslinks.com/compio/jobs